D1167538

small spaces • espacios pequeños
petits espaces • kleine räume

authors
fernando de haro & omar fuentes

editorial design & production

EDITORES   PUBLISHERS

project managers
carlos herver díaz
ana teresa vázquez de la mora
laura mijares castellá

coordination
emily keime lópez
verónica velasco joos
dulce rodríguez flores

prepress coordination
josé luis de la rosa meléndez

copywriter
abraham orozco

english translation
alejandra uhthoff

french translation
angloamericano de cuernavaca; carmen chalamanch tarragona y marta pou madinaveitia

german translation
angloamericano de cuernavaca; sabine klein

design · inside

small spaces · espacios pequeños · petits espaces · kleine räume

© 2012, fernando de haro & omar fuentes
AM Editores S.A. de C.V.
paseo de tamarindos 400 b, suite 102, col. bosques de las lomas, c.p. 05120, méxico d.f.
tel. & fax 52(55)5258 0279
ame@ameditores.com **www.ameditores.com**

ISBN 978-607-437-202-1

printed in china.

index

índice

introduction

introducción • introduction • einleitung

introduction

When we talk of small spaces in architecture, design contributes by giving practical and functional solutions which goal is never leaving aside comfort and the taste of the owners. Using the available space to find the right location for the kitchen, dining room, living rooms, bedrooms, and bathrooms, giving each space its own personality and solutions according with the general style of the house, without losing elegance or comfort, is the merit of a successful design.

Each day there is new and better construction and finishing materials. The same happens in the bath and kitchen furniture industry, where new designs combine materials such as wood, glass, ceramic, marble with innovating, high resistance and easy maintenance coatings, like porcelain and resin. We have to be careful not to neglect the use of new technology in the operation and installation of showers and tubs, and the modern kitchen equipment, which aims to save space.

As well as functional, the small space solution has to be comfortable and hopefully beautiful. It is then that design is essential trying to setup living rooms, dining rooms and bedrooms where personal taste involves deciding the type of materials to be used, like textures and colors.

In all scenarios, decor must assume the leading role, where it can give its dosage of color, joy, versatility, personality and definition of the character of its inhabitants.

Architecture is as important as all the above, it is what produces the livable spaces and their connection; interior circulation and visual contact between different areas; staircases, terraces, gardens, night or natural light and textures.

introducción

Cuando se habla de espacios pequeños en arquitectura, el diseño aporta su propio lenguaje con el que crea soluciones prácticas y funcionales, cuyo objetivo es nunca dejar de lado la comodidad y el gusto de los propietarios.

El mérito de un diseño acertado consiste en aprovechar el espacio disponible para encontrar la ubicación adecuada de la cocina, el comedor, las zonas de estar, dormitorios y baños, y dotar a cada uno con su propia personalidad y las soluciones acordes con el estilo general de la casa, sin perder la elegancia y la comodidad.

Cada día hay nuevos y mejores materiales para la construcción y los acabados. Lo mismo sucede con la industria de los muebles para cocinas y baños, donde los nuevos diseños optan por la combinación de materiales tradicionales como madera, cristal, cerámica, mármol con revestimientos innovadores de alta resistencia y fácil mantenimiento como porcelanas y resinas. Todo ello sin descuidar los avances tecnológicos en el funcionamiento y colocación de regaderas y tinas, así como en los equipos de las cocinas modernas, cuyo objetivo es ahorrar espacio.

La solución de los espacios reducidos, además de funcional, también debe ser cómoda e idealmente se espera que pueda ser bella. Es en esos aspectos donde el papel del diseño es fundamental, sobre todo cuando se trata de acondicionar zonas de estar, comedores y dormitorios, donde el gusto personal interviene para decidir el tipo de materiales que se han de utilizar, igual que las texturas y los colores.

En todos los casos, la decoración tiene que asumir un papel protagónico, en que pueda aportar su dosis de color, alegría, versatilidad, personalidad y definición del carácter de los habitantes.

Tan importante como todo lo anterior es la arquitectura, la generadora de espacios habitables y su conexión; de circulaciones interiores y contacto visual entre diferentes áreas; de escaleras, terrazas, jardines, iluminación natural o nocturna y de texturas.

Lorsqu'on parle de petits espaces en architecture, le langage du design crée des solutions pratiques et fonctionnelles dont leur but est de ne jamais mettre de côté le confort et le goût des propriétaires.

Le mérite d'un design pertinent est de profiter de l'espace disponible afin de trouver l'emplacement approprié de la cuisine, la salle à manger, les zones de séjour, les chambres à coucher et les salles de bains, afin de donner à chaque pièce sa propre personnalité ainsi que les solutions compatibles avec le style général de la maison sans pour autant perdre l'élégance et le confort.

Tous les jours on trouve sur le marché de la construction le finissage des matériaux nouveaux et améliorés ; il en va de même pour l'industrie des meubles de cuisines et de salles de bains, où les nouveaux designs préfèrent une combinaison de matériaux traditionnels comme le bois, le verre, la céramique, le marbre, avec des revêtements innovateurs de haute résistance et d'un entretien facile, tels que la porcelaine et la résine. Ceci sans négliger les progrès technologiques dans le fonctionnement et l'emplacement de douches et baignoires, ainsi que l'équipement des cuisines modernes dont le but est d'économiser l'espace.

La solution pour les espaces réduits, en plus d'être fonctionnelle, doit être également confortable et, idéalement, belle. C'est en relation avec ces facteurs que le design joue un rôle fondamental, surtout lorsqu'il s'agit d'aménager les pièces de séjour, les salles à manger et les chambres à coucher, où le goût personnel intervient dans le choix des matériaux à employer, ainsi que des textures et couleurs.

Dans tous les cas, la décoration doit être la vedette, puisqu'elle doit contribuer sa part de couleur, joie, versatilité, personnalité et définition du caractère des occupants.

L'architecture est aussi importante que tout ce qui précède ; elle crée les espaces habitables et leurs connexions, la circulation intérieure et le contact visuel entre les différentes pièces, les escaliers, les terrasses, les jardins, l'éclairage naturel ou nocturne, ainsi que les textures

einleitung

Wenn man in der Architektur von kleinen Räumen spricht, trägt das Design mit den ihm eigenen Mitteln dazu bei, praktische und funktionelle Lösungen zu finden, die aber niemals die Annehmlichkeit und den Geschmack der Besitzer aus den Augen verlieren.

Die Leistung eines klugen Designs besteht darin, den zur Verfügung stehenden Raum zu nutzen, um die passende Lage für die Küche, den Essbereich, die Wohnräume, Schlafzimmer und Bäder zu finden und jedes mit Persönlichkeit und Lösungen auszustatten, die mit dem generellen Stil des Hauses in Einklang stehen, ohne auf Eleganz und Bequemlichkeit zu verzichten.

Es gibt ständig neue und bessere Materialien für die Konstruktion und die Verarbeitung. Das Gleiche gilt für die Möbelindustrie bei Küchen und Bädern, wo neue Designs auf die Kombination von traditionellen Materialien wie Holz, Kristall, Keramik, Marmor mit neuartigen Beschichtungen von hoher Belastbarkeit und leichter Pflege wie Porzelan und Harzen, setzen. Alles ohne dabei die technischen Neuerungen in der Funktion und dem Anbringen von Duschen und Badewannen und modernen Küchen zu vernachlässigen, deren Zweck es ist, Platz zu sparen.

Für kleine Räume sollten funktionelle, aber auch annehmliche Lösungen gefunden werden, die im Idealfall auch schön sein sollten. Dabei spielt das Design eine massgebende Rolle, vor allem wenn es sich um Wohnräume, Essbereiche und Schlafzimmer handelt, in denen der persönliche Geschmack bei der Entscheidung über zu benutzendes Material, Texturen und Farben, berücksichtig werden muss.

In jedem Fall spielt die Dekoration eine wichtige Rolle, da sie mit einer Dosis Farbe, Freude, Vielseitigkeit, Persönlichkeit und dem Ausdruck des Charakters der Bewohner, ihren Beitrag leisten kann.

Geanauso wichtig wie die vorher beschriebenen Aspekte ist die Architektur, die bewohnbare Räume und deren Verbindungen schafft; sowie Wege im Aussenbereich und den optischen Kontakt zwischen den Bereichen; Treppen, Terrassen, Gärten, Tageslicht oder nächtliche Beleuchtung und Texturen.

kitchens

LIGHT COLORS AND MODULAR FURNITURE IN THE KITCHEN, SUGGEST SPACIOUSNESS, HELP THE CLEANING AND PROJECTS ORDER.

LOS COLORES CLAROS Y LOS MUEBLES MODULARES EN LA COCINA, SUGIEREN AMPLITUD, FACILITAN LA LIMPIEZA Y PROYECTAN ORDEN.

DANS LA CUISINE, LES COULEURS CLAIRES ET LES MEUBLES MODULAIRES SUGGÈRENT UN PLUS GRAND ESPACE, SIMPLIFIENT LE. NETTOYAGE ET PROJETTENT DE L'ORDRE.

DIE HELLEN FARBEN DER MODULMÖBEL IN DER KÜCHE LASSEN SIE GRÖSSER WIRKEN, ERLEICHTERN DIE REINHALTUNG UND STRAHLEN ORDNUNG AUS.

NATURAL AND ARTIFICIAL LIGHT MUST GO SIDE BY SIDE WITH KITCHEN VENTILATION. THE IDEAL LOCATION OF THIS SECTION OF THE HOUSE IS NEAR A WINDOW.

LA ILUMINACIÓN NATURAL Y ARTIFICIAL VA DE LA MANO CON LA VENTILACIÓN DE LA COCINA. LA UBICACIÓN IDEAL DE ESTA SECCIÓN DE LA CASA ES CERCA DE UNA VENTANA.

L'ÉCLAIRAGE, NATUREL OU ARTIFICIEL, EST ASSOCIÉ À L'AÉRATION DE LA CUISINE. L'EMPLACEMENT IDÉAL DE CETTE SECTION DE LA MAISON EST D'ÊTRE PRÈS D'UNE FENÊTRE.

DIE NATÜRLICHE UND KÜNSTLICHE BELEUCHTUNG GEHT HAND IN HAND MIT DER BELÜFTUNG DER KÜCHE. DIE IDEALE LAGE FÜR DIESEN TEIL DES HAUSES IST IN DER NÄHE EINES FENSTERS.

TO HELP THE CIRCULATION IN A ROOM AND THE VISUAL COMMUNICATION WITH THE REST OF THE HOUSE, THE ARRANGEMENT OF FURNITURE MUST BE FUNCTIONAL AND PRACTICAL.

EL ACOMODO DE LOS MUEBLES DEBE SER FUNCIONAL Y PRÁCTICO PARA FACILITAR EL DESPLAZAMIENTO DENTRO DE LA HABITACIÓN Y LA COMUNICACIÓN VISUAL CON EL RESTO DE LA CASA.

L'EMPLACEMENT DES MEUBLES DOIT ÊTRE FONCTIONNEL ET PRATIQUE AFIN DE SIMPLIFIER LE DÉPLACEMENT À L'INTÉRIEUR DE LA PIÈCE ET LA COMMUNICATION VISUELLE AVEC LE RESTE DE LA MAISON.

DIE ANORDNUNG DER MÖBEL SOLLTE FUNKTIONELL UND PRAKTISCH SEIN, UM DIE BEWEGUNGSFREIHEIT IM RAUM UND DIE OPTISCHE KOMMUNIKATION MIT DEM REST DES HAUSES ZU ERLEICHTERN.

A SMALL KITCHEN CAN BE TRANSFORMED IN A BRIGHT AND ATTRACTIVE
SPACE PLACING A LARGE WORK OF ART IN ONE OF ITS WALLS.

UNA OBRA DE ARTE DE GRANDES
DIMENSIONES EN UNO DE LOS MUROS,
PUEDE CONVERTIR EL ESPACIO REDUCIDO
DE LA COCINA, EN UN RINCÓN LUMINOSO Y
ATRACTIVO.

UNE ŒUVRE D'ART DE GRANDES DIMENSIONS
SUR UN DES MURS PEUT TRANSFORMER
L'ESPACE RÉDUIT DE LA CUISINE EN UN
COIN LUMINEUX ET ATTRAYANT.

EIN KUNSTWERK GROSSEN AUSMASSES
AN EINER DER WÄNDE KANN DEN
EINGESCHRÄNKTEN PLATZ DER KÜCHE
IN EINE STRAHLENDE UND
ATTRACTIVE ECKE VERWANDELN.

IN SMALL KITCHENS, FURNITURE WITH POLISHED SURFACE, MIRRORED LIKE FINISHING, LIGHT WEIGHTED, SIMPLE LINE AND REDUCED SIZE, IS IDEAL.

EL DISEÑO ACTUAL DE LOS MUEBLES, CON SUS SUPERFICIES PULIDAS, ACABADAS COMO ESPEJO, LIGEROS, DE LÍNEAS MUY SIMPLES Y DIMENSIONES REDUCIDAS SON IDEALES PARA COCINAS PEQUEÑAS.

LE DESIGN ACTUEL DES MEUBLES LÉGERS, AUX LIGNES TRÈS SIMPLES ET DIMENSIONS RÉDUITES, AVEC LEURS SURFACES POLIES ET LEUR FINITION MIROIR, EST LA SOLUTION IDÉALE POUR LES PETITES CUISINES.

DAS DESIGN MODERNER MÖBEL, MIT IHREN GLATTEN, SPIEGELNDEN OBERFLÄCHEN, LEICHT UND MIT SCHLICHTEN LINIEN UND KNAPPEN AUSMASSEN, IST IDEAL FÜR KLEINE KÜCHEN.

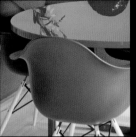

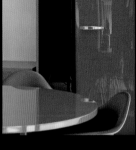

dining rooms

comedores • salles à manger • esszimmer

REGARDLESS ITS REDUCED SPACE, THE DINING ROOM MAY TAKE THE LEADING ROLE IN THE HOUSE AND OCCUPY THE MAIN SPOT.

NO OBSTANTE LO REDUCIDO DE LAS DIMENSIONES DEL ESPACIO QUE OCUPA, EL COMEDOR PUEDE CONVERTIRSE EN PROTAGONISTA DE LA CASA Y OCUPAR UN SITIO ESTELAR.

MALGRÉ LE PEU D'ESPACE QU'ELLE OCCUPE, LA SALLE À MANGER PEUT DEVENIR LA VEDETTE DE LA MAISON ET PRENDRE UNE PLACE PRINCIPALE.

DEM EINGESCHRÄNKTEN RAUMMÖGLICHKEITEN ZUM TROTZ KANN SICH DER ESSBEREICH IN DIE HAUPTATTRAKTION DES HAUSES VERWANDELN UND EINE SO BESONDERE ROLLE SPIELEN.

THE DINING ROOM IS A VERSATILE SPACE THAT CAN BE ADAPTED TO THE DIMENSIONS OF THE SPACE WITHOUT AFFECTING THE COMFORT AND MOBILITY OF THOSE WHO USE IT.

EL COMEDOR ES UN ESPACIO VERSÁTIL QUE PUEDE AJUSTARSE A LAS DIMENSIONES DE LA HABITACIÓN SIN AFECTAR LA COMODIDAD NI LA MOVILIDAD DE QUIENES LO UTILIZAN.

LA SALLE À MANGER EST UN ESPACE VERSATILE ET PEUT S'ADAPTER AUX DIMENSIONS DE LA PIÈCE SANS POUR AUTANT PERTURBER NI LE CONFORT NI LA MOBILITÉ DES HABITANTS.

DAS ESSZIMMER IST EIN VIELSEITIGER BEREICH, DER SICH AN DIE AUSMASSE DES RAUMES ANPASSEN KANN, OHNE DIE BEQUEMLICHKEIT UND DIE BEWEGUNGSFREIHEIT DER BENUTZER ZU BEEINTRÄCHTIGEN.

LAMP SETS, POLISHED SURFACES, DECORATIVE SHELVES AND
ARTISTIC PIECES HELP TO VISUALLY ENHANCE THE DINING
ROOM ATMOSPHERE.

JUEGOS DE LÁMPARAS, SUPERFICIES
PULIDAS, REPISAS DECORATIVAS ASÍ COMO
LAS PIEZAS ARTÍSTICAS CONTRIBUYEN
A ENRIQUECER VISUALMENTE LA ATMÓSFERA
DEL COMEDOR.

LES JEUX DE LAMPES, LES SURFACES
POLIES, LES ÉTAGÈRES DÉCORATIVES, AINSI
QUE LES PIÈCES ARTISTIQUES, CONTRIBUENT À
L'ENRICHISSEMENT VISUEL DE L'ATMOSPHÈRE
DE LA SALLE À MANGER.

LAMPENSETS, POLLIERTE OBERFLÄCHEN,
DEKORATIVE REGALE, SOWIE KUNSTWERKE
TRAGEN DAZU BEI, DIE ATMOSPHÄRE IM
ESZIMMER OPTISCH ZU BEREICHERN.

A LITTLE CHANGE IN THE LIGHT OR A SMALL VARIATION IN THE
TEXTURES CAN GIVE THE DINING ROOM ITS OWN PERSONALITY
AND A SPECIAL ATMOSPHERE.

UN PEQUEÑO CAMBIO EN LA
ILUMINACIÓN O UNA LIGERA
VARIACIÓN EN LAS TEXTURAS BASTAN
PARA DOTAR AL COMEDOR DE UN
CARÁCTER PROPIO Y UNA ATMÓSFERA
PARTICULAR.

UN PETIT CHANGEMENT D'ÉCLAIRAGE
OU UNE LÉGÈRE VARIATION DES
TEXTURES SUFFISENT POUR DONNER
UN CARACTÈRE PROPRE ET UNE
ATMOSPHÈRE PARTICULIÈRE À LA
SALLE À MANGER.

EINE KLEINE ÄNDERUNG IN DER
BELEUCHTUNG ODER EINE LEICHTE
VERÄNDERUNG IN DER TEXTUR
REICHEN, UM DEM ESSBEREICH EINEN
EIGENEN CHARAKTER UND
EINE SPEZIELLE ATMOSPHÄRE
ZU VERLEIHEN.

living rooms

zonas de estar • pièces de séjour • wohnbereiche

A CIERTA EDAD

EL CONOCIMIE

NTO SE LIMITA

A BESOS, ABRAZ

OS Y APAPACHO

S

CREATING BEAUTIFUL AND FUNCTIONAL AMBIANCE, SMALL AND COZY LIVING ROOMS CAN OFFER A PLEASANT VISUAL EFFECT THROUGH FURNITURE LAYOUT AND DECOR.

LAS ZONAS DE ESTAR, PEQUEÑAS Y ACOGEDORAS, PUEDEN OFRECER UN GRATO MENSAJE VISUAL A TRAVÉS DE LA DISPOSICIÓN DEL MOBILIARIO Y LA DECORACIÓN, PARA CREAR AMBIENTES BELLOS Y FUNCIONALES.

LES PIÈCES DE SÉJOUR, PETITES ET ACCUEILLANTES, PEUVENT OFFRIR UN AGRÉABLE MESSAGE VISUEL À TRAVERS LA DISPOSITION DU MOBILIER ET LA DÉCORATION, AFIN DE CRÉER DES AMBIANCES BELLES ET FONCTIONNELLES.

DIE WOHNBEREICHE, KLEIN UND GEMÜTLICH, KÖNNEN, DURCH DIE ANORDNUNG DER MÖBEL UND DIE DEKORATION, EINE ANGENEHME OPTISCHE BOTSCHAFT VERMITTELN, UM SO EIN SCHÖNES UND FUNKTIONELLES AMBIENTE ZU SCHAFFEN.

WHEN CHOOSING THE COMBINATION OF FURNITURE TO ACHIEVE THE DESIRED FEELING THAT YOU WISH TO CREATE ON THE SPACE, THERE ARE NO STYLING LIMITS.

NO EXISTEN LÍMITES ESTILÍSTICOS CUANDO SE TRATA DE ELEGIR LA COMBINACIÓN DE LOS MUEBLES QUE VAYAN DE ACUERDO CON EL TONO QUE SE DESEA IMPRIMIR A LA ATMÓSFERA.

IL N'Y A PAS DE LIMITES STYLISTIQUES LORSQU'IL S'AGIT DE CHOISIR LA COMBINAISON DES MEUBLES QUI S'ACCORDENT AU TON QU'ON DÉSIRE IMPRIMER À L'ATMOSPHÈRE.

BEI DER WAHL DER KOMBINATION DER MÖBEL GIBT ES KEINE STILISTISCHEN GRENZEN, SO LANGE SIE MIT DEM TON, DEN MAN DER ATMOSPHÄRE GEBEN MÖCHTE, EINHERGEHT.

A SMART CHANGE IN TEXTURES CAN CREATE DIFFERENT AMBIANCES
IN THE SAME SPACE, WITHOUT LOSING THE HARMONY OF THE ROOM.

UN CAMBIO INTELIGENTE DE
TEXTURAS CONSIGUE CREAR
ATMÓSFERAS DIFERENTES EN UN
MISMO ESPACIO SIN PERDER LA
ARMONÍA DEL CONJUNTO.

UN CHANGEMENT INTELLIGENT DE
TEXTURES RÉUSSIT À CRÉER DES
AMBIANCES DIFFÉRENTES
DANS LE MÊME ESPACE SANS
PERDRE L'HARMONIE DE L'ENSEMBLE.

EIN INTELLIGENTER WECHSEL IN DER
TEXTUR SCHAFFT UNTERSCHIEDLICHE
ATMOSPHÄREN IN EINEM EINZIGEN
RAUM, OHNE DIE HARMONIE DES
GANZEN ZU STÖREN.

EXCLUSIVE DESIGN FURNITURE, ART WORKS, AND DECORATIVE PIECES MAY FIND ITS PLACE IN A SPACE TO GREET GUESTS.

LOS MUEBLES DE DISEÑO EXCLUSIVO, LAS OBRAS DE ARTE Y LAS PIEZAS DECORATIVAS PUEDEN ENCONTRAR ACOMODO EN UN ESPACIO DONDE SE RECIBE A LOS INVITADOS.

LES MEUBLES DE DESIGN EXCLUSIF, LES ŒUVRES D'ART ET LES PIÈCES DÉCORATIVES PEUVENT TROUVER LEUR PLACE DANS UN ESPACE OÙ L'ON REÇOIT DES INVITÉS.

MÖBEL MIT EXKLUSIVEM DESIGN, KUNSTWERKE UND DEKORATIONSSTÜCKE KÖNNEN IHREN PLATZ IN EINEM BEREICH FINDEN, IN DEM MAN BESUCHER EMPFÄNGT.

EVERY INCH OF SPACE IS WELL USED TO CREATE ECLECTIC
ATMOSPHERES OF GREAT RICHNESS.

EL ESPACIO SE APROVECHA CENTÍMETRO
A CENTÍMETRO PARA CREAR ATMÓSFERAS
ECLÉCTICAS DE GRAN RIQUEZA PLÁSTICA.

L'ESPACE EST PROFITÉ DE FAÇON
OPTIMALE AFIN DE CRÉER DES
ATMOSPHÈRES ÉCLECTIQUES D'UNE
GRANDE RICHESSE PLASTIQUE.

IM RAUM WIRD JEDER ZENTIMETER
GENUTZT UM EKLEKTISCHE STIMMUNGEN
ZU SCHAFFEN, DIE ÜBER GROSSEN
PLASTISCHEN REICHTUM VERFÜGEN.

A FLOOR TO CEILING WINDOW SHOWING THE SURROUNDINGS IS AN EXCELLENT WAY TO GET THE ATTENTION OF VISITORS AND OWNERS, THROUGH COLOR AND TEXTURES.

UN VENTANAL QUE MIRA HACIA EL ENTORNO, ES UN EXCELENTE ALIADO PARA CONSEGUIR QUE EL COLOR Y LAS TEXTURAS ACAPAREN LA ATENCIÓN DE VISITANTES Y PROPIETARIOS.

UNE BAIE VITRÉE QUI SE TOURNE VERS L'ENVIRONNEMENT EST UN EXCELLENT ALLIÉ POUR QUE LA COULEUR Y LES TEXTURES PUISSENT ATTIRER L'ATTENTION DES VISITEURS ET DES PROPRIÉTAIRES.

EIN WANDFENSTER LÄSST AUF DIE UMGEBUNG BLICKEN, ES IST EIN HERVORRAGENDER VERBÜNDETER, UM DIE AUFMERKSAMKEIT DER BESUCHER UND BESITZER AUF DIE FARBEN UND TEXTUREN ZU LENKEN.

THE SMOOTH FLOW FROM ONE SPACE TO ANOTHER HOLDS A DIRECT
RELATIONSHIP TO THE WAY EACH SPACE IS LOCATED IN THE HOUSE.

LA FACILIDAD PARA MOVERSE DE UN
SITIO A OTRO DE LA CASA, GUARDA
UNA RELACIÓN DIRECTA CON LA
FORMA EN QUE SE RESUELVE
LA UBICACIÓN DE CADA AMBIENTE.

LA FACILITÉ POUR SE DÉPLACER
D'UN ENDROIT À L'AUTRE DE LA
MAISON EST EN RAPPORT DIRECT
AVEC LE CHOIX DE L'EMPLACEMENT
DE CHAQUE AMBIANCE.

DIE EINFACHHEIT MIT DER MAN SICH
IM HAUS VON EINEM BEREICH IN DEN
ANDEREN BEWEGEN KANN, MACHT
DEUTLICH WIE GUT DIE LAGE DER
EINZELNEN BEREICHE GELÖST WURDE.

SEE THROUGH WALLS GIVE A SENSE OF AMPLITUDE AND VERSATILITY IN THE SPACE, WHILE CLEAN SURFACES GIVE LIGHT AND HARMONY.

LOS MUROS TRANSPARENTES PROVOCAN UNA SENSACIÓN DE AMPLITUD Y VERSATILIDAD EN EL ESPACIO, MIENTRAS QUE LAS SUPERFICIES LIMPIAS Y TERSAS APORTAN LUZ Y ARMONÍA.

LES MURS TRANSPARENTS OFFRENT LA SENSATION D'UN ESPACE PLUS GRAND ET VERSATILE, TANDIS QUE LES SURFACES PROPRES ET LISSES PROCURENT LUMIÈRE ET HARMONIE.

LICHTDURCHLÄSSIGE MAUERN PROVOZIEREN DEN EINDRUCK VON WEITE UND VIELSEITIGKEIT, WÄHREND REINE UND SAUBERE OBERFLÄCHEN LICHT UND HARMONIE VERMITTELN.

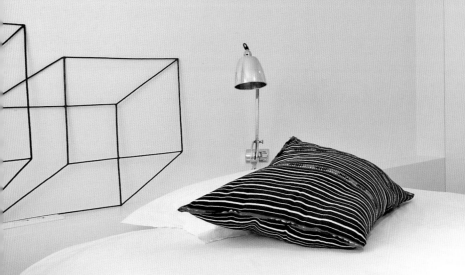

THE COLOR PALETTE AND THE DECORATIVE COMPLEMENTS CAN
VARY FROM SIMPLE TO MOST COMPLEX; THE ONLY LIMITATION IS
GOOD TASTE.

LA PALETA DE COLORES Y LOS
COMPLEMENTOS DECORATIVOS PUEDEN
IR DESDE LO MUY SIMPLE HASTA LO MÁS
SOFISTICADO Y LA ÚNICA LIMITACIÓN
QUE EXISTE AL RESPECTO, ES EL BUEN
GUSTO.

LA GAMME DE COULEURS ET LES
COMPLÉMENTS DÉCORATIFS PERMETTENT
D'ALLER DU PLUS SIMPLE AU PLUS
SOPHISTIQUÉ; LA SEULE LIMITATION
EN EST LE BON GOÛT.

DIE FARBPALETTE UND DIE DEKORATIVEN
ELEMENTE KÖNNEN VON SEHR SCHLICHT
ODER SEHR RAFFINIERT SEIN UND
DIE EINZIGE BESCHRÄNKUNG
IN IHRER VERWENDUNG IST DER
GUTE GESCHMACK.

THE MOST IMPORTANT PRIVATE SPACE IN THE HOUSE IS THE BEDROOM. BY ITS OWN NATURE, EACH OF THEM CAN BE UNIQUELY DESIGNED DIFFERENTLY FROM THE REST OF THE HOUSE.

EL DORMITORIO ES EL ESPACIO PRIVADO MÁS IMPORTANTE DE LA CASA. POR SU PROPIA NATURALEZA, CADA UNO PUEDE DISEÑARSE DE MANERA DISTINTA AL RESTO DE LA CASA.

LA CHAMBRE À COUCHER EST L'ESPACE PRIVÉ LE PLUS IMPORTANT DE LA MAISON. EN RAISON DE SA NATURE, LE DESIGN DE CHACUNE PEUT ÊTRE DIFFÉRENT DU RESTE DE LA MAISON.

DAS SCHLAFZIMMER IST DER WICHTIGSTE PRIVATE BEREICH DES HAUSES. DAHER KANN JEDES EINZELNE EIN SICH VOM REST DES HAUSES UNTERSCHEIDENDES DESIGN AUFWEISEN.

THERE CAN BE MANY VARIATIONS TO THE COLOR PALETTE, FROM BRIGHT, LIVELY COLORS, TO PASTEL TONES AND DISCRETE COLOR ACCENTS.

LA PALETA DE COLORES PUEDE SER MUY VARIADA, DESDE COLORES MUY VIVOS Y BRILLANTES HASTA TONOS PASTEL CON ACENTOS DE COLOR DISCRETOS.

LA PALETTE DE COULEURS PEUT ÊTRE TRÈS VARIÉE, DÈS TRÈS VIVES ET BRILLANTES JUSQU'AUX TONS PASTEL, AVEC DES ACCENTS DE COULEURS DISCRÈTES.

DIE FARBPALETTE KANN SEHR UMFANGREICH SEIN, VON SEHR LEBENDIGEN UND LEUCHTENDEN FARBEN BIS ZU PASTELLTÖNEN MIT DISKRETEN FARBAKZENTEN.

CONTRASTING COLORED WALLS, OR VERY BRIGHT DETAILS IN THE
ACCESSORIES AND FURNITURE, CREATE A RELAXING ATMOSPHERE,
PERFECT FOR REST.

UN MURO DE UN COLOR CONTRASTANTE O
DETALLES MUY VIVOS EN LA DECORACIÓN Y
EL MOBILIARIO, CREAN UNA AMBIENTE DE
RELAJAMIENTO QUE FAVORECE EL DESCANSO.

UN MUR EN COULEUR CONTRASTÉE OU DES
DÉTAILS TRÈS VIFS DANS LA DÉCORATION
ET LE MOBILIER CRÉENT UNE AMBIANCE DE
DÉLASSEMENT QUI FAVORISE LE REPOS.

EINE WAND IN EINER KONTRASTFARBE ODER
SEHR LEBENDIGE DETAILS IN DER DEKORATION
ODER BEI DEN MÖBELN, SCHAFFEN
EIN ENTSPANNTES AMBIENTE, DAS
DIE ERHOLUNG ERLEICHTERT.

CHILDREN'S BEDROOMS DEMAND SPECIAL TREATMENT, WITH BRIGHT AND JOYFUL COLORS THROUGHOUT WALLS, FURNITURE AND BEDDING. DECORATION IS MEANT TO BE VIVACIOUS AND WITH PERSONAL TOUCHES.

EL DORMITORIO INFANTIL DEMANDA UN TRATAMIENTO ESPECIAL, CON COLORES VIVOS Y ALEGRES, TANTO EN LAS PAREDES COMO EN LOS MUEBLES Y LA ROPA DE CAMA. LA DECORACIÓN SUELE SER VIVAZ Y CON DETALLES PERSONALES.

LA CHAMBRE D'ENFANT EXIGE UN TRAITEMENT SPÉCIAL AUX COULEURS VIVES ET GAIES, AUSSI BIEN POUR LES MURS QUE POUR LES MEUBLES ET LA LITERIE. LA DÉCORATION EST SOUVENT PLEINE DE VIVACITÉ AVEC DES DÉTAILS PERSONNELS.

EIN KINDERZIMMER VERLANGT NACH EINER BESONDEREN LÖSUNG, MIT LEBENDIGEN UND FRÖHLICHEN FARBEN AN DEN WÄNDEN UND BEI DEN MÖBELN UND DER BETTWÄSCHE. DIE DEKORATION IST MEISTENS LEBHAFT UND MIT PERSÖNLICHEN DETAILS.

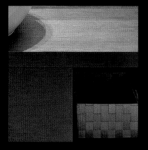

bathrooms

baños • salles de bains • bäder

EVEN IN A SMALL SPACE, A BEAUTIFUL AND PRACTICAL BATHROOM
CAN BE ACHIEVED USING LIGHTWEIGHT MATERIALS.

PUEDE CONSEGUIRSE UN BAÑO BELLO
Y MUY PRÁCTICO, AUNQUE NO SE
DISPONGA DE UNA SUPERFICIE MUY
GRANDE, UTILIZANDO MATERIALES
LIGEROS.

MÊME DANS UN ESPACE RÉDUIT, IL
EST POSSIBLE DE RÉUSSIR UNE SALLE
DE BAINS BELLE ET TRÈS PRATIQUE EN
UTILISANT DES MATÉRIAUX LÉGERS.

MIT DER VERWENDUNG VON LEICHTEN
MATERIALIEN KANN MAN EIN SCHÖNES
UND SEHR PRAKTISCHES BADEZIMMER
ERHALTEN, AUCH WENN MAN ÜBER KEINE
GROSSE FLÄCHE VERFÜGT.

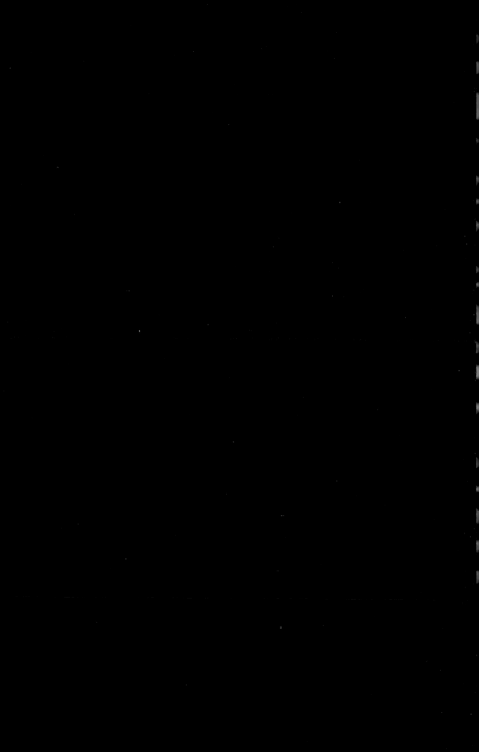

NOT ONLY THE BATHROOM MUST BE FUNCTIONAL, IT MUST BE ALSO
A CHEERFUL AND LIGHT FILLED SPACE, ABLE TO GIVE MOMENTS OF
PEACE AND TRANQUILITY.

EL CUARTO DE BAÑO NO SOLAMENTE DEBE SER
FUNCIONAL, TAMBIÉN DEBE SER UN LUGAR
ALEGRE Y LUMINOSO DONDE SE PUEDAN
PASAR MOMENTOS DE TRANQUILIDAD.

LA SALLE DE BAINS DOIT NON SEULEMENT ÊTRE
FONCTIONNELLE, MAIS ELLE DOIT AUSSI ÊTRE UN
ENDROIT GAI ET LUMINEUX CAPABLE D'OFFRIR
DES MOMENTS DE TRANQUILLITÉ.

DAS BADEZIMMER SOLLTE NICHT NUR
FUNKTIONELL SEIN, SONDERN AUCH
EIN FRÖHLICHER UND HELLER RAUM, IN DEM
MAN MOMENTE DER RUHE VERBRINGEN KANN.

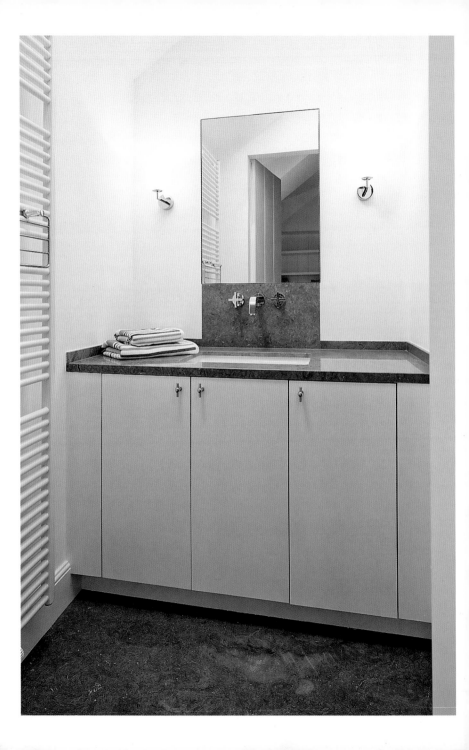

A SMALL BATHROOM REQUIRES LINEAR SIMPLICITY AS WELL AS
MINIMAL FURNITURE THAT MAXIMIZE STORAGE.

UN BAÑO CON POCO ESPACIO
REQUIERE SIMPLICIDAD DE LÍNEAS,
ASÍ COMO UN MOBILIARIO MÍNIMO
QUE PERMITA ALMACENAR TODO
LO NECESARIO.

UNE SALLE DE BAINS AVEC PEU
D'ESPACE EXIGE DES LIGNES SIMPLES
AINSI QU'UN MINIMUM DE MOBILIER
QUI PERMETTE DE RANGER TOUT
CE QUI EST NÉCESSAIRE.

EIN KLEINES BADEZIMMER BENÖTIGT
SCHLICHTE LINIEN, SOWIE EINE
MINIMALE MÖBLIERUNG, DIE ES
ABER ERLAUBT ALLES NOTWENDIGE
UNTERZUBRINGEN.

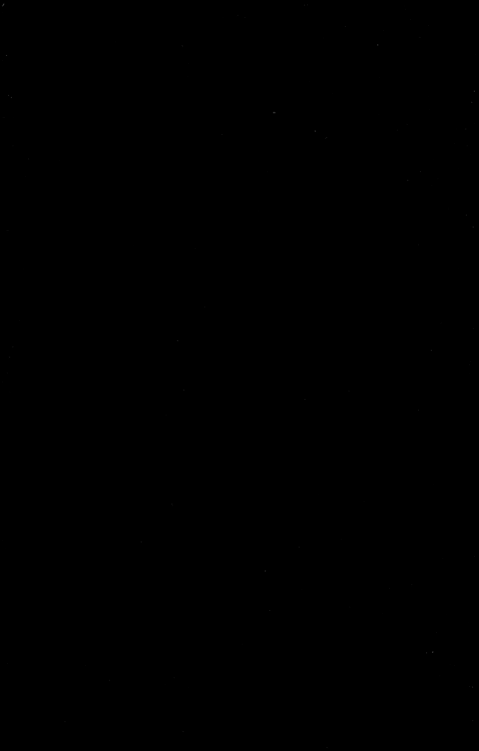

IT IS BETTER TO USE SMALL PIECES TO COVER SURFACES. IT IS BEST TO COMBINE THE ROOM WITH BRIGHT AND LIGHT ELEMENTS WHEN WOOD OR DARK STONE IS INSTALLED.

PARA LOS RECUBRIMIENTOS ES MEJOR UTILIZAR PIEZAS DE TAMAÑO PEQUEÑO. SI SE INSTALA MADERA O PIEDRAS OSCURAS, ES MEJOR COMBINAR LA HABITACIÓN CON ELEMENTOS CLAROS Y LUMINOSOS.

POUR LES REVÊTEMENTS, IL VAUT MIEUX EMPLOYER DE PETITES PIÈCES. SI L'ON INSTALLE DU BOIS ET DES PIERRES FONCÉES, ON PEUT COMBINER LA CHAMBRE AVEC DES ÉLÉMENTS CLAIRS ET LUMINEUX.

FÜR DIE ABDECKUNGEN IST ES BESSER KLEINE STÜCKE ZU VERWENDEN. WENN MAN HOLZ ODER DUNKLE STEINE ANBRINGT, SOLLTE MAN SIE IM RAUM MIT HELLEN UND GLÄNZENDEN ELEMENTEN KOMBINIEREN.

TECHNOLOGICAL INNOVATION HAS CREATED MATERIALS AND
SURFACE COVERINGS MORE ATTRACTIVE AND ELEGANT, THAT IS
WHY THEY CAN BE HIGHLY DECORATIVE BY THEMSELVES.

LA INNOVACIÓN TECNOLÓGICA HA CREADO
MATERIALES Y REVESTIMIENTOS CADA VEZ MÁS
ATRACTIVOS Y ELEGANTES, RAZÓN POR LA
CUAL PUEDEN SER MUY DECORATIVOS
POR SÍ MISMOS.

L'INNOVATION TECHNOLOGIQUE OFFRE DES
MATÉRIAUX ET DES REVÊTEMENTS DE PLUS EN
PLUS ATTRACTIFS ET ÉLÉGANTS, QUI PEUVENT
DONC ÊTRE TRÈS DÉCORATIFS EN EUX-MÊMES.

DER TECHNISCHE FORTSCHRITT HAT MATERIAL
UND BESCHICHTUNGEN ENTWICKELT, DIE
IMMER ATTRAKTIVER UND ELEGANTER SIND,
WODURCH SIE SELBST SCHON SEHR DEKORATIV
SEIN KÖNNEN.

DARK OR BLACK TEXTURES AND COLORS, GIVE A MUCH DEFINED CONTEMPORARY STYLE, WHILE STONE COLORS OR GRAYS CAN GENERATE A VERY PLEASING CONTRAST WITH THE REST OF THE ROOM.

LOS COLORES Y LAS TEXTURAS OSCURAS, O NEGRAS, MARCAN UN ESTILO ACTUAL MUY DEFINIDO, MIENTRAS QUE LAS TONALIDADES DERIVADAS DE LAS PIEDRAS, O GRISES GENERAN UN AGRADABLE PUNTO DE CONTRASTE CON EL RESTO DE LA HABITACIÓN.

LES COULEURS ET LES TEXTURES FONCÉES, OU NOIRES, MARQUENT UN STYLE ACTUEL BIEN DÉFINI, ALORS QUE LES TONS PROVENANT DES PIERRES, OU LES GRIS, OFFRENT UN AGRÉABLE POINT DE CONTRASTE AVEC LE RESTE DE LA PIÈCE.

DUNKLE ODER SCHWARZE FARBEN ODER TEXTUREN SIND ZEICHEN EINES SEHR DEFINIERTEN MODERNEN STILS, WÄHREND STEIN – ODER GRAUTÖNE EINEN ANGENEHMEN KONTRAST ZUM REST DES RAUMES ENTSTEHEN LASSEN.

credits

créditos • crédit • kredit

2-3 Design Primario **5** S+Diseño, Sara Tamez **8** Studioroca **14-15** Arquitectura en Movimiento Workshop **26-27** Abax, Fernando de Haro L. • Omar Fuentes E. • Jesús Fernández S. • Bertha Figueroa P. **35** Agraz Arquitectos, Ricardo Agraz **38-39** Central de Arquitectura, José Sánchez • Moisés Ison **51** Gómez Crespo Arquitectos, Federico Gómez C. **60-61** Cibrian Arquitectos, Fernando Cibrian C. **66-67** Studioroca **70-71** Hidalgo+Hidalgo, Juan Manuel Hidalgo • Rubén Hidalgo **72-73** Ezequielfarca, Ezequiel Farca **74-75** DCPP Arquitectos, Pablo Pérez P. • Alfonso de la Concha R. **76-77** A Creative Process, Andrés Saavedra • Tara Medina **80-81** Mob **89** DCPP Arquitectos, Pablo Pérez P. • Alfonso de la Concha R. **108** Mariangel Coghlan, Mariangel Coghlan **109** Abax, Fernando de Haro L. • Omar Fuentes E. • Jesús Fernández S. • Bertha Figueroa P. **110-111** JHG, Jorge Hernández de la Garza **112-113** Central de Arquitectura, José Sánchez • Moisés Ison **120-121** Abax, Fernando de Haro L. • Omar Fuentes E. • Jesús Fernández S. • Bertha Figueroa P. **122-123** Archetonic, Jacobo Micha **126-127** EXTRACTO Arte, Arquitectura y Diseño, Vanessa Patiño • Robert Duarte **130-133** Studioroca **134-135** Jesús Dávila Architects, Jesús Dávila **136(right)-137** Hidalgo+Hidalgo, Juan Manuel Hidalgo • Rubén Hidalgo **140-141** Arquitectura en Movimiento Workshop **142** Design Primario **143** Mob **146** A-001 Taller de Arquitectura, Eduardo Gorozpe F. **147** Arquitectura en Movimiento Workshop **150 to 153** Agraz Arquitectos, Ricardo Agraz **154 to 157** Kababie Arquitectos **160-161** Abax, Fernando de Haro L. • Omar Fuentes E. • Jesús Fernández S. • Bertha Figueroa P. **164-165** Studioroca **166-167** Abax, Fernando de Haro L. • Omar Fuentes E. • Jesús Fernández S. • Bertha Figueroa P. **172-173** DCPP Arquitectos, Pablo Pérez P. • Alfonso de la Concha R. **174-175** Mob **176-177** Central de Arquitectura, José Sánchez • Moisés Ison **178-179** Design Primario **182-183** Central de Arquitectura, José Sánchez • Moisés Ison **184-185** JHG, Jorge Hernández de la Garza **190-191** S+Diseño, Sara Tamez **196-197** Central de Arquitectura, José Sánchez • Moisés Ison **208-209** Cibrian Arquitectos, Fernando Cibrian C. **210-211** CDS C-CHIC Design Studio, Olga Mussali H. • Sara Mizrahi E. **212 to 215** Picciotto Arquitectos, José Picciotto • Abraham Picciotto • Enrique Anaya • Gabriela Rivera • Mauricio

photographers

fotógrafos • photographes • fotografen